Exposing the Darkness

From a small town where people don't talk or tell

by

Malynda Osantowski-Hughes

with

Kathy Bruins

Foreword

Why on earth did Malynda ask me to write a foreword for her? She could've asked someone important like a Hollywood star, a UN goodwill ambassador. She could've asked any number of law enforcement personnel; we both sit on panels with such as FBI and Home Land Security. It might be the snot I threatened to produce. Maybe it's that I'm a mommy ... that's really all I am. It certainly wasn't the suit and high heels. She says it's because I'm authentic. I looked up the word ... genuine, trustworthy. Isn't that what a mom is supposed to be? Aussie's use the word "dinkum" as a synonym ... sounds better. I think it was the snot.

It was on one such panel that she and I met. It was the usual university setting with hundreds of comfy theatre-type chairs; us sitting at a stuffy table on the stage with name cards to address the audience and answer questions, microphones, a local TV celebrity as moderator; the audience filling in and only five of the six panel members seated. From the corner of my eye, I saw someone slowly coming up on the stage. As she sat with hesitation, she whispered, "I don't belong here. I'm not dressed right."

In my suit and high heels, I immediately whispered, "You sit by me. I don't fit in either. I can blow snot balls from here to the front row if you want." From that moment, we were fast friends. Next time I saw her, she was in the back of the room at another event I'd taken five car loads of staff to. She hung back saying, "I don't fit in." I snarfed her up into our group and guess what … together on our first "outing" in the nastiest part of Detroit, we identified the location of the #1 missing child out of the top 10.

Next time we connected, she agreed to be in our GALA fashion show at the local Convention Center with Miss Michigan, local celebrities, volunteers, a nationally renowned speaker, and 38 rescued women. She chose from our WARdrobe the most amazing red gown you could imagine. She was transformed into a beauty queen, regal, elegant with her dark hair piled high and tumbling down her back. She whispered to me, "You are the first person that has ever made me feel beautiful." Hah. She was born to wear the gown and walk with dignity. It just took a journey and some snot for us to find each other.

That night another survivor started to have a meltdown and Malynda did what she does best … recognized the signs of her own pain, responded with love and wrapped arms of love around a tiny girl once sold to politicians by her dad. She whispered to her, "Never again will you be alone. From this day on, I'm here for you, your own personal circle of protection. I'll do for you, what no one did for me … be there!" The mission statement of Women At Risk, International is just that!

It is my privilege to encourage you to read this story. I have spent three decades in the fight to set the captive free. As the Founder and President of Women At Risk, International, I have the incredible privilege of being the voice of the silenced. Since childhood growing up as an American expatriate in Taliban-type countries, I have seen the many faces of risk. At age 14, in a bloody civil war that my family stayed through … my childhood playmate was raped and fought back. To teach her that she "had no voice," her attackers poured acid down her throat to silence her voice forever. The acid of her suffering became a call on my life to be the voice of the silenced and wrap arms of love around wounded women and children whispering worth and dignity back into their lives giving them a safe place to rewrite the stories of their lives and find their voice. Today we are an organization fighting 14 different risk issues in 40 countries. Because we sell 3000 international gifts of distinction produced by former slaves and at risk women, we are most known for our fight against today's fastest growing arm of crime ... slavery.

Malylnda's story is one of a child ripe for abuse and attack. This is the story of all our children. This is the story of "the land of the free" where the FBI estimates that 300,000 minors (babies to me) are at risk of trafficking a year. New York alone has 3,500 minors for sale ... more children for sale than all the women of all ages that die of breast cancer in a year. This is a carnage of the innocent. This is a cry from a mother's heart to circle your cradle. You can begin by reading this book. Do not be tempted to consider a small detail of her story and write it off as not "your cradle." Malynda speaks painfully into the fact that many minority children in this land are uniquely at risk. Do not think this means your family is safe if you are not a minority. Every story has its own details. This happens to be one of hers, but trust me after three decades of fighting this … all children are being hunted in this land of liberty that we so love. I could recommend another ten stories to read that take this one detail out. Listen to her story. Memorize the lessons she has learned. Lean into what that means in your own circle of influence. I am calling you from the deepest recesses of my heart to read this book in order to become a circle of protection to your own babies and those you love. That is what Malynda wants. She would like someone to "be there" for your babies like no one was for her.

So, this mommy (a 30-year veteran in the fight for freedom), and a thriver (she's so beyond just surviving) named Malynda continue to turn stories of pain into stories of rescue and hope to compel you to gather courage and take action to be a circle of protection to those in need. I'm proud to give voice to Malynda. I'm so proud of her journey to find her own voice that culminates in this book. Malynda, you are my hero. But, I'll beat you at blowing snot balls any day!

Becky McDonald
President of WAR, International

INTRODUCTION

An engine's sound made me jump. I cringed knowing the horrific nightmare would continue. Each car that pulled into the driveway meant pain for me to endure. When the car door slammed, my heart stopped and I found it difficult to breathe.

I heard him enter the house, and hoped to be forgotten. He would call my name. When I went downstairs in fear, I knew that I would not be getting a gift or a gentle hug from someone who loved me, but their hands gripped me, either my stepfather or someone he brought home with him, forcing me to go into the bedroom, undress and do things a little girl should never have to do. I hoped every day never to hear that engine come in the driveway. A car accident killing him instantly was what I wanted.

I believed this to be normal family behavior and couldn't understand how other children could smile and laugh. What was wrong with me? I felt sad all the time. It was years later that I discovered this was not normal behavior in the home. How could I not know? I was trapped in a cycle I thought hopeless. However, God has healed me and given me strength to tell my story.

My hope is not only to help those trapped in the sex trafficking industry, but also to help communities be aware of the evil that may be in their midst. The truth is kept in dark places where no one talks about it. Victims, wounded and filled with shame, tend not to tell anyone, feeling they have no voice. Much was stolen from their lives. I want them to realize there's a chance of redemption. They can stand up to the evil, and recognize their true identity.

My story is also for readers who have never experienced or known much about sex trafficking. A community that becomes aware can help victims heal as well as help get rid of the evil.

I hope for a better world where children no longer are treated as a commodity. Adults need to be educated on how to recognize it and what to do to prevent it. The innocence of a child will no longer be stripped of them if we as a society unite in eradicating this wickedness.

The abuse many children and youth have experienced forms a self-belief that they are too messed up ... too far gone. That lie is keeping them in chains. By me breaking the silence and escaping the dungeon I was left to be locked in for the rest of my days, it is like shining a light into their darkness of the truth that they can be free. God's truth can do that. They will be set free, the prison doors opened and the chains broken. God's Word says there are two things that defeat the powers of Satan: the Word of God and the truth of your testimony.

Throughout my story, I share with you poems and letters I wrote as a form of therapy. I believe these will give you insight to the emotional pain I experienced along with the healing God was doing in me.

God has done a wonderful work of healing in me, making me want to reach out to others who are enduring and suffering in this horrific crime that is plaguing the children in our cities and hometowns. Victims come from any economic status, race, gender, or locality. No one is immune.

Join me in exposing the darkness of abuse and sex trafficking. I pray that my story raises your awareness as well as heightens your hope in a solution. There is hope.

CHAPTER 1

A vision of a dirty ragged little girl came to me as my husband was driving the car. We were both praising God as worship music echoed from the radio, when I stopped singing. I saw clouds surrounding the little girl. The distressed child had been crying. The dried trail of tears that streaked down her dirty little face told the story of her hard life experiences. Her arms and legs were bruised, her little body was obviously all wounded and bleeding. The child's eyes appeared swollen shut. This poor little girl looked to be hurting terribly. Obviously, she had been traumatized by circumstances, ravaged with the worst life had to offer. I felt sorry for her, I tried so hard to just look away from her, but I could not look away A part of me wished I had never seen her.

The girl's face looked so familiar. I could not place

where I'd seen her, yet deep within me I knew I should know her, but I couldn't place how, why or when I met her. Frightened by her condition, I found that I didn't want to know her. Why would I be scared by a wounded little girl who needed help? Could I admit my fear was not so much what I was seeing, but the familiarity I had avoided for years? The knowledge I buried so no one would ever know that the girl was me.

I looked at my husband and he was smiling and jamming out to D.C. Talk singing "Jesus Freak," completely clueless to what was going on in me. The vision continued for me—this time I was floating towards the girl. Within seconds, I was no longer looking at the girl, but looking out from her eyes.

As I looked through her eyes, I saw God's throne. It was massive and beautiful beyond description. I could not see His face, but felt God's arms lift me onto His lap. I recognized His voice which comforted me, as did His arms around me. He laid me upon his lap, and placed His arm under my head. All I could think about was how dirty and wounded I appeared, and I could not believe He put me upon His lap. It was almost as if He could read my thoughts.

He said, "Look, baby girl ..."

I tipped my head up a bit and glanced down at my clothes and skin. The dress I was wearing became so bright white; no longer dirty or ripped. My arms and legs had no evidence of wounds or bleeding anywhere. How could this be? I looked towards His face, and although I couldn't see it, it felt warm and comforting. His love for me flowed through me like a river rushing over me on a 102-degree day. I had never experienced this before in my life.

God then said, "Malynda, my child, I desire to heal you. I need to go into every wound you experienced and remove all foreign debris that doesn't belong there. Allow me to mend these areas in you, and you will no longer be hindered from healing. You, my daughter, will no longer have to carry the pain."

For comparison, God then used a memory to demonstrate the cleaning and healing that I needed. My husband had once caught fire as he was pouring gasoline into a carburetor. Flames engulfed his arm, and his son and I threw dirt on him to put out the flames. At the hospital, the nurses said his burn had to be cleaned thoroughly so infection would not set in. They used a wire brush—one that looked like the type we used to clean grill grates—to get the dirt and gravel out of his arm. They placed that wire brush directly on the burned area and scraped it up and down.

His screams reminded me of nails scratching across a chalk board. It broke my heart, I felt so helpless. They said if they didn't do it, gangrene might occur and eventually work its way through his body. He could potentially loose a limb or worse.

With great compassion, God told me that cleaning my wounds would be very painful, like the process of cleaning my husband's arm. He said the stones of shame, pain, anger and hurt needed to be completely removed so they would not spread through me and destroy my being. As an example, God showed me a septic system. When you first have an issue, it seems to be in a certain area, but soon it is backing up into your sinks, washing machines, showers, and everywhere. Debris from years of damage, if not removed from me and cleansed, would be evident in many areas of my life.

The Lord asked if I would be willing to be cleansed and made whole.

"Yes."

Clueless to what the journey would entail from the healing process, I knew that God desired the best for me. My trust for Him wasn't fully developed, but there was a surety in His Love for me.

God explained that the process would be one wound at a time. He said an incision made inside of me allowed the infectious matter to run out. Then the cleansing occurred with the precious blood of Jesus, like a power washer going deep into the wounds within me, pushing up the debris exposing the hidden stones. Next, the healing balm of Gilead and the comfort of the Holy Spirit filled the wound. (The "balm of Gilead" is a reference from the Old Testament, but the lyrics of the spiritual "There is a Balm in Gilead" refer to the New Testament concept of salvation through Jesus Christ. The Balm of Gilead is interpreted as spiritual medicine that is able to heal Israel and sinners in general.) Like any surgery, it was painful, but needed for true healing.

He asked me again, "Do you want to be healed?"

"Yes, my Lord."

The days following this commitment, I noticed things that never bothered me before. Certain smells sickened me. Seeing men playing alone with little girls nauseated me, even in their innocence.

One day as I drove, my healing began. A man came in a vision I knew as a child. He laid on top of me forcing me to engage in oral sex. I smelled the stench of his sweat, the excretions of his body fluids, and felt the gagging response

16

in my mouth. Shaking down to my soul, I stopped the car and began to pray. I wept and screamed from the agony. The pain felt as if inflicted on me right then. The painful experience slowly diminished by the comfort of the Holy Spirit. The Spirit flooded my car with the scents of frankincense and myrrh removing the odors of my vision.

I heard God whisper in my ear, "I am with you. I will never leave you nor forsake you."

True healing began. This journey drained me of self, and gave me no choice but to rely totally upon God.

I imagined a few months of the intense surgery and healing the Lord would bring, but little did I know it would actually expand into years. I definitely was not at Burger King and getting things my way. The smells from my past abuse panicked me before I realized their origin. It would be the same with certain words I heard or how they were said. If I touched or saw something that reminded me of my past, a memory triggered, and the childhood horror I experienced came back to mind. I had no idea that triggers activated by the smells, images, touches, and audible things I heard causing my insides to cringe, feel sick, and afraid. When I had them, they would send me into a panic attack.

I kept myself trapped in a cycle of abuse by reliving the experiences in my mind. That horror needed to be cleaned out. I held it all deep inside of me where no one would find it, or so I thought. God knew it was there all the time. He saw me becoming a prisoner in my own created cell. The key to opening the cell and being set free was in the healing.

I was unaware of what is known today as Post Traumatic Stress Disorder (P.T.S.D.), which is a mental health condition that's triggered by a terrifying event, either experiencing it or witnessing it. Symptoms may include flashbacks, nightmares, and severe anxiety, as well as uncontrollable thoughts about the event.

Symptoms of intrusive memories regarding the traumatic events included recurrent, unwanted distressing memories, reliving those moments as if they were happening again (flashbacks), I had upsetting dreams, and experienced severe emotional distress and physical reactions to something that reminds me of the events.

At first, I didn't know how to handle all that was revealed to me in memory. Some days I held onto a thread of the hem of Christ's garment fully aware He was holding onto me. The pain felt unbearable at times, as if I could physically die. God's loving arms cradled me through the toughest times. The moments I felt the weakest actually became the intimate moments of learning more about God and His promises.

I had to be broken down. In the breaking, I learned to overcome by realizing it would not be done in my own strength, but in God's. I give God all the glory for the healing He did for me. I would never have brought myself down this journey had I known all that it included, and therefore, would have never been healed. My life today is so much better than I could ever imagine it. The healing began for the dirty little girl—the rag doll—whose life was brutally traumatized by the evil of adults, and now comes out of the shadows to be the princess God intended.

God has made Himself known to me for the purpose of showing His love to me, healing me and giving me purpose … what a blessing. Here is how I met Jesus.

CHAPTER 2

In 2001, I was driving down I-69 taking my daughter to her dad's. We had just newly separated and I was at the end of giving life a try, when all of a sudden a vision appeared to me. I saw an electric blue silhouette of Jesus standing in an archway holding his arms wide open with a beautiful rainbow of colors glowing behind Him.

I kept hearing him say "Come."

Frustrated, I said, "I don't know how! Take me now … beam me up!" I was totally convinced that the only way to Christ meant I had to be dead.

When I arrived at my daughter's dad's home, he wasn't there yet, so we went in. I turned on the TV, tried every station, and adjusted the rabbit ears, but the only station I could get to come in clearly was channel 28, a local Christian station. A lady on the television said, "Are you trying to figure out how to get to Christ? I'm going to help you."

I could not believe what she said, I wondered how she knew that. I put the baby down. Giving her my full attention. She said, "Repeat after me. Father God, I believe your son Jesus Christ died for my sins and I ask You to forgive me of all my sins, I receive Your forgiveness and invite Your Holy Spirit in to empower me to walk out this salvation. Satan I renounce you and all you have been in my life. Thank you, Father God, for forgiving me, in Jesus name, amen."

I prayed that prayer, and after doing so, I felt absolutely no different. I was frustrated in believing that I didn't get it.

Then it was almost as if she knew what I was thinking, because she said, "To seal this, you have to find a local church and tell them you just got saved and you need to be baptized. After doing so, all the old will pass away and all will become new."

Great! There is one more step to do. My daughter's dad arrived and I left to go talk to a women who worked at the Turning Point Shelter. She reminded me of the lady on TV. I told her about my experience in praying the prayer. She congratulated me on my decision and agreed with the lady on TV encouraging me to go to a church and get baptized.

That night, I went out and medicated my frustration the way I knew how. I got drunk at a local bar, which was a far cry from a church, but it was Saturday and everyone knows there were no local churches open for business. The next morning, with hangover and all, I woke up and found a church in the neighborhood.

I went to church first thing after I got ready. Greeters welcomed me at the door. I told the lady at the door I needed to speak with the pastor dude, and get that baptism thing.

She said, "You can't do that. You're not sanctified. You've got to go through some classes before you can talk to the cardinal pastor."

I said, "No, no, no, you don't understand. The lady on TV said that after I pray the sinner's prayer, Jesus comes into my life. Jesus makes me righteous and holy. I need to be baptized for the old to pass away and all things become new."

She says, "No, it doesn't work like that."

I say, "You know what, you can just go to fricken hell, lady." I was totally pissed off. I left the church.

A few days later, I drove to a doctor's office. I told him I needed some serious drugs, because I was ready to start hurting some people. It was the first time I had ever asked for medication. He wrote me a prescription for Xanax, and gave me free samples to take while I was there.

So I bought a fifth of Jack Daniels and a pint of apple pucker, along with already taking the samples the doctor gave me.

The next day, a friend called me and said he was given a saw mill and asked me to come work there.

My good dad had a stroke recently, so I decided to drive there to help care for him and check out the saw mill.

That night, I drove over to my mom and good dad's house to stay the night. I had a dream about doves landing on a building. One died and one stayed. I had no clue about the dove in relation to Jesus yet. The image was so real in my mind as if it really happened. The next morning, I went to the saw mill, and when I arrived, it was the same building the doves landed on in my dream. No one was there yet, and I had my daughter with me. I set up the pack and play for her and lit up the wood stove to make it warm in the room. There were two knocks at the door. I opened it and the man said, "Malynda?"

I said, "How the hell do you know my name?"

"Jesus told me."

I said, "Oh hell no, I don't qualify for Him. I done tried and I ain't qualified for Him, been there, did that, so you

23

can take your Jesus crap and just get the hell out of here, because I ain't about to go through all that bullshit again. I tried everything. I have said the sinner's prayer, went to a church and got kicked out. I'm done."

He said, "Can I pray for you?"

I said, "You do your heeby-jeeby thing and then you can get the hell out of here."

He began to pray and said, "I bind whatever is hindering you from receiving the gospel of Jesus Christ. In the name of Jesus."

All of a sudden, every negative thought vanished from my mind. I was thinking, Wow! Not one cuss word, not one thing bad was in my mind. It was amazing. I asked him if he knew anything about the baptismal thing.

He said, "Yes, I do."

I said, "Let's do it." It was the day before Easter Sunday, snow on the ground and freezing cold. I said, "I want it now."

He asked, "Now? It's really cold out there."

It did not matter to me. I knew a place right down the road that stopped at the creek. So we drove there. The bridge was completely bent up in the air so you could no longer cross the road. It seemed to be a sign from God to me saying that once you took this road, there was no going back. He baptized me in that cold water. Something changed inside of me. I could feel it.

The pastor wanted me to meet a lady, who was a member of his church, at the local gas station in the morning, so that she could show me how to get to church. When I met her in the morning, she was furious with me saying, "I had an Easter special planned for today and you made me late. If it were not for my granddaughter, I would have left you here."

I said I understood and that I was there, so let's go. So I followed her to the church.

When we arrived, I sat in the back of the church. I was looking at everyone as much as they were staring at me. The place was packed. They all had skirts down to their ankles, no make-up, and I considered them holy people. I was feeling totally freaked by this, let alone making the little old lady late for her Easter special she planned. She was one uptight chicky.

Next thing you know, the little old bitty stood behind the pulpit, and I thought she was about to explain why her lateness for the Easter special. I totally wanted to duck and hide. Instead, it was worse. She said, "I had an Easter special I planned for today, but we know how God is and He has canceled my plans and told me I am going to sing a song to a very special girl, his daughter." The next thing you know, she was pointing at me. I really wanted to hide, everyone stared at me, bandanna, the only thing holy about me was my jeans.

She began singing a song called "Alabaster Box" by CeCe Winans. She got to the place in the song where it said, "When she walked in the room everybody stared, and even her parents said this is no place for someone like you." It was at that moment, I felt like someone picked me up and carried me to the front of the building. I wept and wept as she sang the song.

I remembered a time when Jesus came to me as a child and said, "I am sorry your parents chose to treat you the way they have, and one day, I am coming back for you, and you will be able to choose. In my mind, I felt He came back for me. He kept His word. This was the first time I had ever known that kind of loyalty. I felt real love for the first time in my life. At that time when people came around me, it was as if Jesus would rise up inside of me and make me feel all nice and loving, when I knew that I naturally wouldn't be that way towards them. I looked at people as if they were taking up oxygen that I may need to breathe one day, I had absolutely no time for them.

I fell in love with my Prince that day. It was the most

amazing day of my life. He was faithful and came back for me. I felt a love like no other. I was in love.

CHAPTER 3

A memory was coming to mind as I laid in bed. It was nearing the end of summer. My husband and I enjoyed an evening together sitting upon the rocks at the end of the pier. We shared with each other our feelings about the worship at church that morning. In God's love and intricate ways, He ministered to both of us. It amazed me how God dealt with each of us so differently, but yet in a way that made us both feel significant, like we were the only ones in the world.

My husband knew I was drained from all that God did in my life, even though my husband never dealt with that type of hands-on healing before with someone. He felt intimidated, which was difficult for him as well. God knew my husband was the right person to handle the job, because though he lacked in some understanding, he stood strong and faithful to intercede for me, even into the wee hours of the morning. He was an amazing man of God.

On our way home that evening, the Holy Spirit began depositing gifts in me, upon the Father's request. Like the gentleman Jesus is, He asked me, "Will you receive the gift of prophecy?"

"Yes."

Then He asked, "Will you receive the gift of healing miracles?"

"Yes."

He asked, "Will you receive the gift of intercession?"

"Yes."

This continued, and with each gift I received came an anointing poured on me. For each gift, it felt as if liquid warm oil ran through me like peace, total peace flowing through me. That is the only way I can describe it. Then He anointed me with the ability to laugh at His enemies, which is also known as the gift of discernment.

He gave me joy in abundance that night, all night long. My husband and I laughed, loved and shared. Words cannot describe the awesomeness of what God had done. Prior to this, I endured what seemed like weeks of anguish intense surgery, delivered with a spiritual surgical knife in the hands of the ultimate Physician. The long overdue night of refreshment for my husband and me brought a feeling of victory knowing soon there would be more.

A few days later, the memory came with intensity and felt like it was happening at that moment. I could see the blood rushing from the eyes, ears, nose and mouth of a little girl under 2 years old. A woman wiped away the blood, pressing on her chest and breathing into her mouth, as the man who caused the wounds stood by.

I heard the Holy Spirit reveal to me that I was the little girl. Instantly, I was inside the child looking out eyes swollen shut, and still hearing Jesus talk to me letting me know I was safe. Then I began talking as if I was handicapped mentally. Jesus then removed the demonic spirit that was attached to me at that time of mental retardation. His Holy Spirit exchanged it for a spirit of wisdom and knowledge. At that moment, I realized Jesus saved me from mental retardation I should have had due to the physical abuse I endured.

I received confirmation of that truth in memory. The woman who was my nurse and brought me back to life several times, as well as my mom, when she finally shared the truth, told me everything about it. She said I was beaten so badly that it was a week later before she saw the hand-print formed on the side of my head. My gratitude to God for not allowing the weapon formed against me at that time to prosper.

The same night, God revealed to me memories of being forced to watch men sexually assault animals, dead ones, and they made me lay in the blood as I was sexually traumatized. I was revolted in this memory. I could not stop vomiting or rid of the overwhelming panic. The Holy Spirit embraced me with comfort and a peace that passes understanding allowing the deliverance from a spirit of bestiality.

It's obvious that this section is difficult to share, but from my experience, that is a sign true healing needs to be done, but really, true healing has been done. That is why I struggle with this section. I am a normal human being and the thought of anyone doing these things to a child disgusts me.

I remember being made to lay next to a dead deer as they gutted it describing how they would gut me if I didn't eat the raw meat. As I ate that meat, I thought that it tasted better than their kissing my lips and shoving their tongues and penises in my mouth. Experiencing this, I knew it was more than deer that suffered this fate.

Once my mother's husband realized my hiding spot with the pigs. He came in and tried doing a sex act with my pig in front of me. That pig picked him up by shoving his head underneath his body and literally threw him about 20 feet. I watched as he killed the pig. Forced to watch, I cried. He then stripped me naked and laid me on my dead pig and sexually assaulted me.

After this happened, one of the men who came and stayed at our home watched what happened and participated as well. He left that day and when he came back, he brought me a Miss Piggy doll and told me, "This is to remind you of what will happen if you tell anyone. You will be killed like the pig." He was new, so I guess he felt the need to threaten me. I didn't understand what he meant.

That was a memory God took that night. He revealed it and totally healed it.

I had experienced these types of events from ages 13 months to 13 years old with my mother's husband. There were also multiple men he knew who forced me to do sensual things with them, so it is understandable the blockage of memories in which I escaped.

My husband wept when I endured this type of healing for he had difficulty hearing about everything. I always shared what God was doing, what I saw, and could see how difficult it was for him to hear. He cried with me. So many nights, I wished healing would end. I could not handle it at times. During the healing, parts of me would rise up and run from seeing any more, for I was being traumatized all over again. This made our relationship one that was off and on, in and out. But thank God, my husband was a rock. He never wavered knowing that God was working in me. My husband was a true warrior who stood in the gap for me.

Though many people did not see our relationship as good, it was more of a God-thing. My husband loved me like Jesus and though I only shared a few memories of my reality of hell as a child, we endured years of this war, which was for me. My husband fought right alongside of me for my freedom. He stood against the devil in Jesus' name as Christ did, with all authority of God's Word as a weapon used to fight Satan's dark activities against His wife. No matter what I did, he knew that I was sanctified through him. My husband said that he takes God's Word to the bank. He stood for me for seven years, and two years after, I lost him in an auto accident. I answered the call to set the captives free, loving people like Jesus, as my husband and Jesus loved me. So like all the people in the Bible, I was somebody, too, and God took me in knowing I was unqualified and He qualified me.

In His righteousness, I stand healed, whole and restored beginning the new chapters of my life in Him.

Amen.

Finally, brethren, whatever things are true, whatever things are noble, whatever things are just, whatever things are pure, whatever things are lovely, whatever things are of good report, if there is any virtue and if there is anything praiseworthy – meditate on these things (Philippians 4:8 NKJV)

I Couldn't Breathe

By Malynda Osantowski-Hughes

I couldn't breathe,

I couldn't breathe,

Gasping my breath,

I could hear you scream

Do what he says,

You better listen to your daddy

Listen to what he says,

I was a good girl,

I didn't cry

I didn't scream

I couldn't breathe

I couldn't breathe

Not allowed to speak unless

Spoken to.

Can you not see what you did to me?

It was as if you laughed as my vocals were ripped from me.

My voice was silenced,

I was locked walls of hell,

The torment never seized

You mommy seen, you my mommy, look what you done to

me, you watched me bleed,

You seen the feces run down my legs,

You looked at me in disgust as if it was my fault.

I was forced to submit to…

I couldn't breathe!

You seen mommy, but you never heard,

You seen me mommy, but you never heard.

CHAPTER 4

My bedroom door squeaked open. I knew that sound well as a five year old. My stepfather chose me that night. I heard his footsteps getting closer to my bed. Pretending to be asleep would do me no good. Fear overwhelmed me for there was no escape. If I cried or vomited from the nausea I felt, it would be worse for me. No matter how many times this occurred, each time, I endured the shivering of fear to the core of my being—that never changed.

He lifted my blankets and laid on me. From his weight crushing my little body, I couldn't breathe. The excruciating pain he inflicted caused me to black out. When I awoke, blood and stool were wet underneath me, and I smelled the foul odor of the man who hadn't bathed in weeks.

I got out of bed, sore from the abuse, and cleaned myself with an old shirt. Even at this young age, I had become numb to this treatment and no longer cried.

Even if I wanted to, the tears wouldn't come. I felt nothing. I believed life was hopeless for me, because I became accustomed to this experience and knew it would happen again and again. I believed all kids went through it. I hated it.

On school days, I awakened with the desire to get to school as soon as possible and away from the house. In the morning, I got myself something to eat, usually a bowl of cereal or a glass of powdered milk. Then I dressed in old dirty clothes from the day before and left the house. No one said good-bye to me—no one cared if I went or not.

I waited in front of the house for the bus. We couldn't afford boots, so I always wore my tennis shoes. Once on the bus, I would go straight to my assigned seat. No one wanted to sit with me anyway, so I was thankful for assigned seating. As I walked to my seat, the kids held their noses as I passed them and laughed.

"The animals in my barn smell better than you."

Kids were quite cruel. Strangely, their negative comments never bothered me.

Even so, I loved school. It was an escape for me. Even if sick, I went to school just to get away from home. I didn't have any friends, but school was still better than home. I avoided staying home at all cost.

I was a loner, I never talked much with anyone. Danni, a girl with whom I shared a locker, sat in the same assigned seat on the bus with me, and we had the same classroom. She always tried getting me to talk more. Danni told me how her grandma had the same name as me, and felt it was God's way of showing her she had a guardian angel.

Danni and I never really talked about our lives. She shared some about her family. They seemed very loving, and I wished I were her.

How could Danni be so happy all the time? I believed what happened to me at home occurred in all homes, including her happy one. I thought my abuse was normal. I never feared anyone finding out, because I thought it was common knowledge. I spent my days in sadness most of the time. I believed something was wrong with me, because everyone else, especially Danni, seemed to be happy.

Danni tried hard to include me in what she did, but I didn't feel worthy. One day, she brought her lunch into the girl's bathroom where I went like clockwork every day at noon. I loved being able to run the hot water on a paper towel and wash my face.

Danni came in to the girl's bathroom. "Malynda, would you like to share my lunch?"

I screamed at her. "What do you want from me?" No

one ever did anything for me without a cost. I believed she was like everyone else, wanting to get something from me.

Danni cried. "I just wanted to share my lunch with you, that's all."

Danni went home that day and shared with her mother what had happened. She cried because she wanted her mom to rescue me. It was clear to Danni something bad was happening to me at home.

The next day, Danni and I were in class and a kid put his hand on my shoulder. "Are you okay?"

I freaked out and ran out of the class room. The teacher asked Danni what happened, and she told her.

"She freaked out in the bathroom when I was being nice to her the other day, too." Danni told the teacher about the many bruises on me. She also said she saw me cleaning up blood from my skin.

The teacher came and found me in the bathroom. She brought me back to the class and sat me down to do my work. When recess came, the teacher asked me to stay in class, so I did. The teacher introduced me to a police officer. They began asking me questions and I answered them truthfully.

As I answered them, the policeman began crying. I was shocked at the tears. I asked him, "Why are you crying?"

He said, "Mommies and Daddies are not supposed to do those things to children."

I was furious, because even though I truly believed that it happened in everyone's home and I was just a sissy, deep inside there was a feeling that it was not right. To hear a man say this with tears in his eyes, blew my mind! I had never seen a man cry. When I get home, I would tell my family that this was not supposed to be happening. I was so mad!

The officer then explained what normal families do. In my mind, I compared my family. During meal times, our family sat around the table together. It wasn't a happy time, and sometimes I was forced to eat an abundance of food and sometimes very little. I was seldom allowed to eat the same food as the adults.

After dinner, if my name didn't get called to do the dishes, I knew my fate. I would be forced to go into a room or shed and perform sexual acts by my mother's husband or one of his friends who stayed at our home.

I was not the only child in the home, though I do not desire to share their experience. The reality of seeing them led away to the same torture I experienced was more painful than enduring it myself. I was not allowed to watch television. It seemed that any type of communication with one another or the outside world was prohibited. I would silently do chores. I was not allowed to speak, cry, or feel. Any movement frightened me, especially unexpected ones—I easily jumped. My anxiety as a child made me feel sick many times. I developed full blown shingles at age 11.

I remembered a video camera being in the room as I performed sexual acts with different men. The same two or three men abused me, except when I was taken elsewhere, then it would be other men. In the early years of my childhood, I was trafficked before the term became well-known.

No safe places existed at our home. I would hide with the pigs and talk to them. They were my only friends. I had some chores which included tending the pigs. I loved seeing the new pigs that came every month. Looking back, I never thought about the odor in that pig pen. There is a pig farm not too far from where I am today and the smell of it is horrific. It blows my mind that I found that comforting as a child.

I laid there for hours and really didn't want to leave them. They comforted me. I knew once I left them, it may be a while before I could visit with them again. I was not allowed to roam by myself too often for they wanted to keep control over me at all times. Although I couldn't escape physically, my mind provided a way out. My mind could take me a million miles away. I dreamed of taking my siblings far away from that place and all living together in a place happy and safe.

My parents had a very small circle of friends and didn't socialize much. I suppose they wanted to keep the secrets of what went on at home quiet. There were no family gatherings or reunions. No one came over unless they participated in the abuse that went on. If that weren't enough, many times I was sent to my mother's husband's family and forced to perform sexual acts of all kinds. I was not a person, but a commodity.

One set of friends my parents had never hurt us. They were special to me. I felt safe there. They had three daughters and we spent a lot of time with them, but it never stopped what was going on at home. I wonder why my parents took to these people and not others.

Once there was a male at these friends' house who forced his hand into my pants. Although that probably sounds horrible to many, it was the least of what I had endured as a child.

We cut wood with this kind family. I would be in the woods for hours at a time working, but also admiring the trees around me. It felt like a safe place with the trees being my guards. I pretended to be a princess living in a tall tower where nothing would hurt me. Reality would come back much too soon, as a piece of wood flew through the air hitting me and knocking me to the ground. I was then instructed to get back to work.

Christmas was never a happy time. As other children waited with anticipation for the day to arrive, I only dreaded it, mostly because it meant I was forced to stay home for days and days. I received only a couple of token presents from relatives who lived far away. No family ever visited. I wonder if they suspected something or just didn't want to be involved with the family. The dysfunction ran rampant through our family and I'm sure was sensed by others.

Most Christmases were awful. A group of men came to the house for one thing. Christmas was horrific just like any other day.

My birthday was celebrated twice in my childhood, and I hated them. My mother's husband used them as a reason to beat me with a board and give me a pinch to grow an inch.

I also received more trauma, and I wanted to be dead. Keeping my siblings together and desiring to protect them was what kept me going in life. I imagined myself taking them away from all the hurt and pain. I dreamed someone would come into the house and rescue me from it all. I was so desperate for freedom, but clueless to if it existed.

In comparing my family to what the officer was telling me about normal families, it was obvious the wrong my family did to me, and it made me angry. His interpretation of family and mine were very different.

I went home on the bus that day. When I arrived, my mom was in the kitchen in the basement, and her husband was just getting home. Before I could get down the stairs to tell my mom what I learned, because in some self-protecting way, I believed her clueless in knowing she was not supposed to be allowing these things to happen.

Before I got down the stairs, I heard her husband call my name. I slowly turned around and headed back up the stairs. Walking over to remove his boots as I was required, I stooped down to grab a hold of one. As I removed his boot, the words of that officer were welling up inside me.

My mom's husband began to fondle my privates with his foot. I pushed him away and ran down stairs screaming to my mom, "The officer said he is not supposed to be doing that to us no more!"

My mom looked at me as if she had seen a ghost. My siblings began screaming at me to shut up. My mom went

45

upstairs to her husband. Moments later, she told us to put on our coats and shoes and get into the car. We did, but the silence was eerie. It felt like we were in that car for hours. They took us to her husband's parent's home and dropped us off. His parents were not abusive physically, but horribly mentally abusive.

My mom and her husband left, and it would be a couple days before they came back to take us home. The next morning after being home, we rode the bus to school. When we arrived, we were instructed to go to the office. When I got to the office, the officer and teacher were there with my mom. My mom had been instructed to remove me and my siblings from the home or they would.

My mom took us to Detroit, Michigan. I was so happy, I truly believed the cop told my mom the truth and she was clueless to how a family functioned. When we arrived at the home in Detroit the first night, we slept and I was so happy knowing it was over.

The next day, my mom took us to get haircuts. She said it was so her husband could not recognize us. My sister got a perm, my brother got a normal haircut, and my beautiful and long hair was chopped to my ears. I could not get a perm or regular cut, because he would be madder at me, because I was the one who told.

Shortly after being in our new location, there was a new man that showed me what it was like to have nice sex. He explained to me how mean the other men had been in my life. If there was any hope in me, it was completely drained at that point. A woman began taking me to an alley in the worst parts of Detroit and leaving me in the car. Men came out and forced me to perform sexual acts. My voice was stripped—there was not one ounce of hope left.

My mom received a letter in the mail from the court saying we were not needed to testify against her husband due to overwhelming evidence. Her husband was sentenced to 5-15 years in prison.

We moved shortly after back to the place my childhood horrors began. Moving back seemed so difficult. I will never forget the feeling of everyone's stares as I walked down the halls at school. Inside, I cringed at the thought of everyone knowing what my home life was like. It was the first time in my life I realized that my childhood was not normal. The shame that I held within me felt like thick nasty tar … no matter what I did, it wasn't washing off.

When we arrived, my mom, siblings and I lived in a little apartment. I kind of felt like a women getting out of a convent. I became completely defiant to any rules. I attended school, but skipped and fought as much as possible. I did not have many boyfriends. I learned through the questions of other kids that I was not a virgin and I did not want to explain why.

One day, I decided to skip school with a friend. We walked to the park and saw a few of the bad boys in school hanging out near an antique caboose. They were destroying it—kicking the windows and pulling the seats. One boy shared how his dad was an alcoholic and beat his mom bad last night. I could see the reason for his anger and pain.

Needless to say, these guys were obviously used to this sort of thing, because when the cop pulled up, they were gone. The cops asked me who did this damage.

I told them that I did.

They looked at my 97-pound frame and asked if I was sure?

"Yes, I am sure that I did it."

They put me in the cop car and took me to the station. When I arrived, one of the bad boys showed up and declared to the cops that he was responsible. I could not believe the kid everyone said was bad was standing up for me; no one ever did before. Expelled out of school, I was made to live at my mom's boyfriend's home.

My mom's boyfriend had a son who I met when I first arrived. When we were alone upstairs, he convinced me to come into his room. Honestly, I didn't mind for he was just a couple of years older than me and cute. We began to make out when my mom walked in and saw what we were doing. She began shouting at me, "You little whore! You ruined one marriage; you will not ruin another one!"

She then took me to my grandpa's house about 20 minutes away, where I was made to live in the garage. I was not allowed in the home due to the fact my mom made me out to look like the worse child ever to my grandfather's wife.

My mother never came to see me. I lived off $30.00 worth of food stamps my mom sent once a month. I lived off Doritos, M & M's and Mountain Dew.

I continued living there for a few months. I missed my siblings terribly.

I had joined the track team at school, which I was never required to attend practices because I was one of their top runners. One day, I told my step-grandmother that I was going to practice. She never really cared where I went; she didn't want me living at her house anyways ... even if it was in the garage.

So instead of going to practice, I began the journey to walk 20 miles to see my siblings. I was determined.

On the way there, I was picked up by a man I was

regularly trafficked to as a little girl. I have no idea why I got into his truck. I was in the middle of nowhere and he was the only vehicle on the road. The only other reason is the damage that had already been done to me left me hopeless to find help, so running wasn't an option in my mind. I never even considered it. It seemed at that point no matter where I went, sexual trauma was a lifestyle.

The man forced me to perform sexual acts and then dropped me off at my mom's. I had bloodstains all over my friend's yellow jeans I borrowed and looked bruised and swollen from crying.

When I opened the door, I fell down to my knees crying. My mom grabbed a belt and began beating me, hitting me over and over. I cried out begging her to please let me stay with my siblings. I promised to never say another word if anyone ever did anything to me, if she would please let me stay.

My mother allowed me to stay at that time. She was getting ready to move into her boyfriend's house.

My mom started sending me at the age of 14 to Detroit on the weekends. The words I spoke to her echoed in my mind in that I promised no matter what happened to me, I would never say another word again, not to anybody. I could not bear the thought of not being with my siblings.

The bond I had with them goes beyond words.

Bloodstained Sheets of Innocence

By Malynda Osantowski-Hughes

The wounds initially

Raged within me.

Numbness was not an option

Daily reality raged within me,

Bloodstained sheets of innocence,

Bloodstained sheets of innocence

Upon me grown men, upon me beast raping the very innocence of my soul,

They stripped my innocence forced to perform forced to display

The very innocence of childhood, I never seen, I never had.

From a baby, learning to walk, unable to talk…

Bloodstained sheets of innocence

Bloodstained sheets of me,

Torn and tormented, cuts and wounds,

Shattered bones, mouth ripped open,

Anus and vagina split in two,

No doctors, no stitches, it's a miracle I'm alive to say,

Though you tried to steal my identity,

You never won,

The memories used to haunt me,

I would shut my eyes to hide,

Trying to ignore the reality

Of who you were of who all played a part of trying to destroy

This precious soul,

Today I stand,

Because of the innocent shed blood of one

I now am free, I am free.

I am healed, I am restored,

The scars of your damage

Are evident,

But the wounds, oh those wounds,

How deep they went,

The river of God's love,

Went deeper and made me new,

Innocent shed of blood,

No longer am I a stain upon a sheet,

I am me!

I am free!

I am free!

CHAPTER 5

I'm fourteen and awaiting my ride to the city. Instead of this being an exciting time for me, I dread it knowing what is waiting for me in the city. My mother is sending me to people's home, a place I would love to believe she was unaware of what was happening, but that was not the case.

A woman picked me up. My very first night there, that woman made me get undressed and lay in her bed. She said if I did not do it, her husband would kill both of us.

She stared at my body telling me how deformed it was, and that her husband may not even want to touch me. She spread my legs apart looking at my privates and mocking me. Her husband soon came in. Ignorant in his speech, he began forcing himself in my private areas. By this time in my life, there were no screams or tears. He became angry that I was not a virgin and called me a whore and other vulgar things. I laid there numb. He told his wife that I would do and to get me ready.

They do not treat me as a child, but as an item of merchandise. New rules apply here, and if I don't obey, I will be killed. They want me to primp with red lipstick, darker blush and dark eye colors. When I look in the mirror, it's hard to see the 14-year old girl. Prior to this, I was never made to wear make-up. In the mirror, I saw a puppet that moved to the commands of the evil puppeteer. There were no good people in this world.

At this time, my mom and I lived with the man she married. He seemed very nice, but my barriers weren't lowered just yet. Many others in my life pretended to be nice and suddenly turn very mean. Bobby could be another. Clearly, Bobby was clueless to what took place when I was taken to the city. I knew for certain I was not to mention anything to him. Living in the garage of my grandfather again and never seeing my siblings was the last thing I wanted to happen.

As the days went by, I felt Bobby was a good guy. He never hurt me, and treated me nice. I found myself trusting him more. At our meals, we ate the same thing as the adults.

Occasionally, men came into our home when I was alone and force me to have sex with them, claiming a debt needed covering. No matter what happened to me, I was persuaded that my voice no longer existed. It seemed there was no safe place for me. When my mom's husband was home, no one ever came over and did that stuff. But the weekends came and it would be back down to the city again.

I had a serious fear of these people. I remember being made to watch one of the men that hung out in the city hold a gun to a young boy's head and pull the trigger. His brains and blood scattered all over the place. A cop showed up and never asked a question, just shook the guy's hand, and put the body in a body bag. They threatened me and my family, if I did not do what they said.

These people took me to the street races, where we stood on the corners watching the cars and advertising our merchandise. I watched them release an African-American man in the road telling him to run. One of the two cars racing hit the guy and his body ripped in half. They left him lying in the street.

Afterward, they took me to a house party with lots of men of all ages. I was forced to drink and take drugs. All I remembered was waking up in the morning naked. I had nasty stuff coming out all over me. A lot of times, I didn't remember what really happened. I went home on Sunday, and Monday I went to school. This became my normal routine.

Bobby's son, Ricky, who lived with us, found the pills I was forced to take daily at home. The reason being, according to the woman, they did not want me getting fat.

Ricky showed me the pills he found and wanted to talk about it. Buzzed by the drugs, focusing on him was difficult.

He started yelling at me. "Where the hell did the drugs come from?"

I was scared to answer.

"I promise not to tell anyone. What are they doing to you?"

I was freaking out knowing if I told, I could be forced to live back in a garage and never see my siblings again.

He would not stop asking and demanded I tell him.

I broke down crying, begging him not to tell my mom. He listened to everything that happened and became furious.

"She will not make you go live anywhere. My dad will not allow it." He waited for my mom to get home and began yelling at her like I had never heard anyone yell at her. "You better never send her down there again! If you do, I am going to tell my dad every fricking thing you have done!"

Ricky kept me home from school. He sat down next to me on the couch. "You will feel sick. Don't be scared. Your body will be detoxing from the drugs."

Soon, I began vomiting and shaking horribly. My veins felt like fire. Sweating profusely, I had no idea what drugs from which I was coming off, but I knew I never wanted them again. After a couple days of this, it was over. I was so thankful for Ricky at that point in my life.

To my surprise, my mother never made me go down to the city after Ricky confronted her.

After I stopped being trafficked in the city, I had a friend who wanted me to go to a motel with her. She actually was not a friend. She knew the drug dealers, who sold to the guys who hung out with my new older stepbrothers. She said she needed me to go with her to a motel, and that it was urgent.

When we got there, we went inside. She picked up an eight ball of cocaine. (I did not do drugs, but due to all the trafficking in my childhood, it was obvious to me what it was.) She left the building telling me to wait right there and she would be right back.

Two big tall guys who were a lot older than I came into the room. They ripped off my clothes and began simultaneously having sex with me. By the time they were done, I was barely breathing. They put me in a tub with very hot water.

The girl came back and acted as if she had no clue those guys were going to do that to me. I will never forget showing up for school Monday, walking up to the girls who were her friends and punching each of them in the face. They all knew what happened and thought it was funny.

To me it seemed there was no escape. It was as if I was destined to live this way. Many abusive situations happened to me. I tried to have a boyfriend, and sadly, the reality that I was not a virgin and enduring other sexual trauma made it difficult. I had a crush on a guy who was clueless to what happened in my home. It was obvious that he liked me, but the closer he got to me, the more I pushed him away and ignored him every time he arrived. He wasn't mean to me, but I was convinced that I was damaged goods, and no one would want me if they knew the truth. It was painful to see him with a girlfriend, but I felt like spoiled goods.

My sister and I went to Wal-Mart with a friend of hers. While there, she and her friend had stolen lots of stuff. I didn't know about this.

When we got outside the store, a man called out to us. My sister quickly handed me stuff out of her pockets. They took us up into a room and began questioning us. The police were called, and we got a ticket to show up in court for shoplifting.

My sister and I left, and she still had a purse full of stolen cassette tapes. They never knew she had them.

When we went to court, my sister was placed in a foster home and I was put on probation. I went to visit my sister at her foster home, and they were amazingly nice people. My sister liked them a lot.

I got the idea that I wanted to go to a foster home too, especially if they were as nice as these people. I knew if I ran away, I would have to report to my probation officer. Well, I did run away, and the judge asked me why. I told him, I wanted to go into the same foster home as my sister. They allowed me to live there, and then moved my sister to another one.

I was overwhelmed with the love there. Ironically, the foster home was in the same school district from which I had been rescued less than three years earlier. I returned back in the same grade as when I left.

My mom had visitation every other weekend. On the way back from visiting my mom, we had driven by our old home and outside in plain sight was my mom's ex-husband who trafficked me.

"Stop the car!" I shouted. "I want to see my dad!"

This was a result from what I later came to know as a trauma bond—a much distorted view of relationship. My mom stopped the car. There was no response from the man except, "I cannot talk to you."

I got back in the car and when I arrived back at my foster home, I told my foster mom what had taken place. She got tears in her eyes and said, "Honey, he is not your dad. That man did horrible things to you."

I was upset and yelling at her. She then told me, "Honey, I can show you the medical documents from the doctors."

I broke down crying wanting to know why I wanted to see him. She told me that my mom should not have brought me to see him. I could not believe he got out of prison so early; only three years he served.

My foster mom and I bonded more during this time. She spent a lot of quality time with me, making my mom very jealous and mad. Visits with my mom became accusations of how horrible my foster parents were, how they acted like they were better than her.

It came time for my stay to end at my foster home. I was allowed to stay at my friend's the weekend before my release to go home. I really didn't want to go home. My friend and I snuck out of her house and walked to her boyfriend's.

When we arrived, we decided to take the car. My friend made out with her boyfriend while I, all of 4 foot 6, decided to drive while they made out in the back seat. I drove in the county where my foster dad just happened to be a police officer. Needless to say, an officer followed me the whole way, and come Monday morning, I spent my birthday at the courthouse. I didn't know what was going to happen to me. I was there for hours and hours.

My foster mom picked me up and took me home to their house. This was the first time my foster dad participated in my life. I will never forget the shock of it. He was furious with me.

I had an attitude that was so bitter and said things out of spite. He sat me down and told me I was a manipulator and messed up. I was not shocked by his analogy for it was obvious to me I was messed up. I didn't realize how bad until I lived with them and experienced normal life. The impact he made in my life from that day on was powerful.

My stay was extended and chores were made to cover the cost of fines if I received a ticket for real. Running red lights, no license, no turn signals—the list went on and on. It was in that situation, I knew the compassion of a family.

Looking back, I see that my foster dad had absolutely no idea how to deal with a wounded traumatized child. But the key penetrating my heart was their love.

My six months there went fast. My foster parents and siblings were not home the day I was picked up for good. They said it would be too hard. Their relatives lived right next door and were watching from their house to see my mom pick me up. That was the hardest day of my life. I truly loved those people.

Malynda's childhood pictures

Malynda's childhood home

CHAPTER 6

Living at my mother's house after leaving the foster home was a change I didn't want to make. I tried to make the best of it.

More trauma came into my life through men that continued to abuse me. I became pregnant and forced into many horrendous situations. I loved the new life that came from me … somebody to truly love and protect. I wanted a better life for my child. At this time, I didn't know how to make that happen especially since my self-esteem was very low. I couldn't see myself successful and good for only one thing.

I tried to escape my life and survive by going to my cousin's house where I was trafficked as a child. She was the only family I had from which to get help. She told me I could strip and make money to get out of my situation.

I started to strip. I got drunk because that's the only

way I could do it. The next day, I said to myself, if I cannot do this sober, I'm not doing it. I went to a party where I was scheduled to perform. There were 300+ people at this bachelor party. I sat down and started to cry. The guys let me stay and I made about $3,000 just sitting there with them. They didn't force me to dance or anything.

More trauma occurred as I continued to find a way. At this point, I was getting angry. I was tired of being walked all over. I wanted it to change.

I went to a school to get my GED and degree as a clerical medical assistant. I was receiving a 4.3 grade point, which I felt so good about. I was excited about graduating. However that too was short lived. The school went out of business a day after graduation and I along with many others did not receive the GED or degrees we earned. Defeat once again came.

I decided to enter construction with the idea that I could get tough and whoop a man, if needed. I lived in fear of certain men for years and I was tired of it.

One day I was watching the Oprah Winfrey Show. She shared stories of women who never knew they were abused. As I listened, their stories defined mine. Oprah encouraged everyone that if they were in these kinds of situations, they needed to get away. I was living in a bad situation like this right then.

I was clueless. I had an aunt who lived near me and I asked her to watch my son when I worked. I also had a friend who held onto the money I made, because I didn't want the man I was involved with to get it. He found out and after a violent exchange, I was able to get away, but never totally away. I always feared for the life of my son and me. This fear lasted many years. When I thought he was out of my life, he would find a way to get back in to torment and traumatize me.

Years later, I was married to a Christian man. At that time, I had my son and a daughter. We had a wonderful marriage. I loved him very much.

In 2006, we were in a severe car accident that took my husband's life and injured my son and me terribly. My son had massive head injuries and I began to have seizures the days shortly after the accident. A girl had run through a stop sign and hit us.

With his head injuries, my son could not travel for more than an hour away from the destination. I could not drive because of my seizures, so I had to leave my son with family. There was a strain in the relationship with this family, so I wasn't able to talk to my son for some time. I would leave messages on their machine for him, but I wasn't getting a response.

Sometime later, I began to hemorrhage a lot, put in the hospital and given four pints of blood. I called my son and left a message that I loved him so much.

He called back and said I was never in his life and that he hated me. You see, his brain injury erased a lot of memories of me. But when he said he hated me, all hope drained out of me.

Would true freedom ever come?

* * * * * *

Losing people I love hurt so much. Bobby and I became close over the years. I called him Pops. On December 21, 2006, 20 years later, I look back at a time when we were in the car and he was talking to me about God. He told me the reason he never got baptized was his fear of water. He never really liked God at all, because his mom went to church all the time, but she was really mean and threw his little brother out in front of a truck. He said nobody ever did anything about it. She told him God was punishing him and if we were going to be bad, God would punish us, too. Bobby could not see living for a God that mean.

When he saw me work things out, he realized God's not like that. He saw Jesus in me in a way he had never seen. He knew my childhood trauma to a degree that put my mom innocent and her ex as soul abuser, and how I had overcome through so much. He said he was proud of me.

He knew I had just lost my husband and he would have given anything to take away that hurt. He knew God did a miracle in my son. He saw so much love and many miracles in my life, but there was something he said bothered him for years.

"What is that?"

"I don't understand why you never trusted me."

I was shocked. How could he even think that? "You're the only man I ever trusted." He's the only one I had been alone with and thought was an amazing guy.

He cried. It was a touching moment. I knew I meant the world to him, and at the same time, he finally knew he was my world.

He dropped me off in town. "Why don't you come over for hamburgers later?"

"Thanks, but I'm going to just stay home and wrap presents."

Not even five minutes later, I received a phone call that he was in an accident. That was so hard for me. In 2006, just before Christmas, this good dad, the only great one I had, died in a car accident. It still pains me to remember that day. His goodness gave me hope.

I see now that my relationship with Bobby was a gift. He was an expression of God's love for me and showed me that there were good men in the world. Through him, my narrow aspect of what life was about opened up to better things for me. It was so difficult for me to recognize and receive love from anyone, but I learned as the healing process was happening, and I am still learning.

Because of You, Lord

by Malynda Osantowski-Hughes

There was a time I thought I could never endure,
The only thing I could do was fall to my knees and pray,
Through all the trials
And through all the fears,
I know, dear Jesus, You were near,
Grasping on Your garment
Through Your grace alone I endured.

Here I am, through the battle scars remain
I came so far
My faith is stronger than before.
Here I am, I made it through
Here I am, Lord, glory to You
I could never doubt Your love for me anymore.

I am no longer what I believed to be true
A little whore born to be abused
There were times I had not one friend
An outcast that just didn't fit in
When I didn't handle things the way I should
I can look back and see I never understood

Now I can see Your Mighty Hand
How You God took something bad and made it good

Now today I stand in You with purpose
Here I am with no fear
Through these tears
My faith is stronger than before
Here I am, Lord, thanks to You
I have endured, I have triumphed
In the victory of Your grace attained for me.

I will never doubt Your love for me anymore
Thank You, Lord, for never letting go
For being faithful to finish
The work You have begun
I am here, Your Word is true,
It does what it's sent to do
Weeping may endure for a night
But joy comes in the morning.

CHAPTER 7

It was not long after that God had dealt with me with forgiveness. My mom and I had begun to communicate and healing was taking place. I wrote about my feelings in the form of letters to my mother and perpetrators. Here is one I wrote to empty my feelings out on paper.

Mom,

Though you were not willing to share the fullness of the secrets you kept, at this point, I truly did not know if there were secrets or if you had blocked the trauma that you allowed in your children's lives.

To make a long story short, it took years for healing to come, but I have overcome, Mom. What I once thought was never possible to do, became possible through Christ, and I know you are aware of the journey I have come through.

It was not until 2008 when you finally told me you were sorry you never got to know me, because you allowed Satan to steal every chance by hiding under the shame of your choices. For that, I have forgiven you and so does Christ, but until you could forgive yourself and face the truth of your choices and allowing God to change your heart through repentance, I could no longer have anything to do with you. That was the hardest day of my life, but the greatest as well. It hurt bad to have to face the reality that you would probably never be the mother I hoped and dreamed for years you would be, and it was painful to let go of all that anger that raged as God took me through more healing, showing me all the damage that had been done. Although I knew in my heart it was God's divine timing, I was broken that day, but when I walked away from you, God lifted years along with tons of burdens from me. I had never felt such liberty.

I was not worried of upsetting you, nor was I afraid of never having you. I was free. I no longer had to live a delusional life pretending you were some wonderful mother in fear someone else may see who you really were and find out what my life was really like. I was free!

God did not stop working in both of our lives. You went back to where you lived and an angel showed up at your door as a biker dude and said, "God sent me here because someone needed a ride to church."

You stood up and said, "That would be me."

I will never forget hearing your testimony to your cousin that following week. You shared how we had talked at the hospital, how for the first time you had known that you knew you were forgiven, that at the hospital that day when I had told you what I said and walked away, that you saw Jesus in me that day, and you gave your life to God and are now free. I cannot tell you how much I have wept for the work Go had done in you, but it was not until the day I was asked to share my testimony of Child Exploitation that I knew that God had truly changed you. You shared with me how important it was to get my story out there so no other children had to go through what I endured. You stood by and supported me even during the news interviews and you did it with such a grace of God knowing you were free from the sins you allowed in your life. I was never so grateful in my life.

I am so thankful to God, that the true miracle that happened for me was seeing the desire change in my heart for you. I no longer wanted you to pay for what you had done and allowed in my life. I truly wished to see you have everything you have never had. You were the mom I never thought could be. You showed me that taking accountability for our failures as a parent can change one's life perspectives forever. I am still in awe.

I rejoice, because for the first time in your life, you have a man who desires to show you love and does so daily. That encouraged me that one day, I will know that love from a man and all in God's timing.

I can say I have no anger, no hate, no "ucks" whatsoever when it comes to saying and knowing you are my mom. God broke me from the Stockholm Syndrome that made me feel guilty of your actions and gave me the desire to make excuses for what was, and when He did I was set free and so are you. I love you because I love you. I see you how Jesus sees you and would be the first to shut down any other talk You still today know what I do for a living and encourage my passions in exposing the darkness of this crime, and I pray that if there are other victims who have had this problem with their mother that it gives them hope to know God can do anything. With proper timing and God's divine hand in restoration, relationships that were once unhealthy and destructive holding so much rage and anger can be healed. I am grateful you chose to be accountable and receive Jesus' blood that was more than enough to cover even your sins.

To my perpetrators,

I also say to the rest of you who have been perpetrators in my life, I have forgiven you and released you into God's hands and if I never see you, I know and believe through the power of prayer each and every one of you will see me in Heaven, because God will answer my prayers. God's Word says He will avenge His children speedily and seems we do not war against flesh and blood buy principalities and powers. I know that I know. God have given me the necks of my enemies and you aren't my enemy, the demons within you are and I declare and decree God's warring angels to minister in behalf of your salvation. I come against the demonic principalities that have ruled your life, and not by my might nor by my power, but by and through the Spirit of the One and only true and living God. The Lord rebukes you Satan out of every area of their life in the name of Jesus, and I invite the Holy Spirit into their lives opening their ears to hear the Spirit of God and to no longer heed any other's instruction, in the name of Jesus. I say this because God has given me the necks of my enemies, may you walk in liberty and turn from your sins and never, never come back to them, in Jesus name.

Love a once victim, who became a survivor and exceeded beyond thriving and has been transformed into a reviver. You no longer have anything in me … nothing. I have released you to my Lord and Savior Jesus Christ.

CHAPTER 8

My mother was also sexually traumatized in her own life. Does that justify her old choices? No, not by any means. I too endured a horrific childhood.

My mother struggled and still struggles with memory blockage like I did. To her, it was a hopeless cycle. She learned the cycle and believed that was her life. I believed the same. As I came forward with my testimony, she realized that she had a voice, too. All those years, she never realized she had a voice. To me, that was an inspiration.

At first, she felt only shame for her own life as well as her kid's. She now encourages me to use my voice. I wish I knew her story long ago. It's the perfect example of why people need to know about the cycle of abuse and that it is not right. Now one of my strongest supporters, she has awakened to the truth of what happened to her and what she allowed in her children's life. I believe she blocked a lot of the things that happened because it was so traumatic for her.

My mother also suffers from Post-Traumatic Stress Disorder (PTSD). I thank God for the triggers that helped me see what happened to me was wrong. She never experienced that insight. She has repented of it, and the only thing she feels she can do is encourage me to come forward.

My siblings are supportive, for they too have been through a lot of trauma. I do not share a lot about it, because that is their story. We have this unspoken rule to not talk about it, but we also know we have each other's back.

My brother is very excited. He said, "God is doing some serious cartwheels and back flips knowing how much it took to get you where you are now. We both know it was way worse than you even remember."

It's wonderful to hear the cry of the heart of each other, along with other victims and survivors who are going through similar trauma.

I am speaking for all children and my family. Sex trafficking is all over the world, not just small towns. Many generations suffer this same cycle. When I became a Christian, I believed what God said regarding generational curses.

> I, the Lord your God, am a jealous God,
> punishing the children for the sin of the parents
> to the third and fourth generation of those who
> hate me, but showing love to a thousand
> generations of those who love me and keep my
> commandments (Exodus 20:5-6 NIV).

That's why I strive, lay in His arms, and hold onto His promise—I have children. I don't want to see them go through the generational curses that I've been through. I could never be in the position of not knowing whether it is right or wrong. I can't blame my mom for what she didn't know. Growing up, I was traumatized and literally thought that people around me were happy about that being in their life.

I hated my mother for years. Then God dealt with me about the forgiveness. The first time I called her out on the issues, she was in the hospital. My daughter asked her why she was so mean to her daughter.

My mom said, "It never happened."

I had papers from the prosecuting attorney of my mom's husband. My daughter showed the papers to her grandmother when she came home from the hospital. They had gone outside. My mother had just had heart surgery and still had stitches and wires on her chest. When she came back in, the chest incision was opening up and she was feeling really sick. I took her to the hospital and after I came home, my daughter told me what she said. I was shocked.

I was praying about what to do. I went up to the hospital with my friend, Tammy. When I walked in her room, I felt led to tell her, "I am so sorry that you allowed shame to ruin any opportunity of knowing me as your daughter. I am an amazing kid. Someday, when you realize how much Satan has pushed you into feeling guilt and shame and all the lies that come from the pit of hell, and you come to know Christ and receive that forgiveness as much as I have forgiven you and He's forgiven you, and you get rid of that shame, then maybe one day we can be a mother and daughter. Until then, I want nothing to do with you." I left the hospital.

God supernaturally had her transferred from the hospital in Fremont to Mt. Clemens, which was four hours away. That never happens. They took her by ambulance. The next day, I felt like hundreds of pounds were lifted off of me. It was amazing.

Earlier during my healing, my mother told me that what I was seeing was a lie, and never happened. A couple weeks later, my mother accidentally hit a man on a motorcycle and he died. She lost her vision. I was helping her to find the insurance papers for her accident since she was not able to see. She handed me some papers thinking they might be it. They were not insurance papers, they were the prosecuting attorney papers from Jackson prison.

I was shocked. I read on the papers, "multiple variables of abuse and there was no need for the children testifying because the evidence was overwhelming." All that confirmation of what God was revealing to me through the triggers to healing was hitting me all at the same time, right after my mom had told me it was a lie and never happened.

I remember I left her house, went to a cabin across the state and cried for hours. I really believed the things I went through weren't from God. I thought it was something demonic, because I didn't remember the fullness of my childhood. It was easier to believe my mom that it never happened than to realize how pathetic and horrible it really was in my life. When I got the papers, it was like truth, evident and overwhelming, in my face.

These were the same papers my daughter found that

day she brought them out to my mom who had denied to her that she ever hurt her children.

I remembered some of my teenage years, but a lot of my childhood, I do not remember. I had to talk to my younger brother who remembers everything. I was telling him how I got the papers and how they made me upset.

He said, "I want you to know that what you remember is not half of what happened to you. You ought to be thankful that God's only shown you some." He also said, "If you stay focused on what you are doing no matter what, and skip the parties here, you will make it through. Remember that when you get to heaven, we will all be there, because you kept going."

We are going to have the biggest party ever, knowing what he endured was beyond my imagination. How could a boy go through that? Women think we get traumatized, yes, that's one thing, but having that happen to a boy by multiple people, to me that was overwhelming. That thought alone pushed me to overcome.

My biggest inspiration was my little brother and my sister saying to me, "You can do this. Don't quit now. We need you."

During the process of writing this book, I talked to my sister. She made a statement to me when I was struggling after a local detective came against me hard for sharing my testimony. He told me I was doing it for sympathy and I was worse than an infidel as a mother for broadcasting it. He said many horrible things.

I was ready to quit, and my sister said, "Listen, if you shut up now, then he wins. Be like you were before God; be a bitch. God did not want you to coward down, so stand up. You are sharing not only your voice, but ours too and many others."

My sister also remembers bits and pieces, because she experiences blockage like I do. It confirmed my memories of what they went through, too. I do not talk a lot about it with her except once she said what really bothered her is that our mom acts like she really never knew. She hates that about my mom. I said the trauma sometimes is overwhelming for her, too. She didn't know how to fix it for herself, so how could she fix it for us? It truly makes it difficult to share the depth of my healing with them.

CHAPTER 9

It's amazing how God takes the horrible things in life and turns them into beauty (Isaiah 61:3). One day, I went over to my old house where my landlord's son now lives. He allowed me go upstairs, and I looked out the window I did so many times as a child and took a picture. He then took me to the shed, where many horrible things occurred. He knew what happened to us as kids, but he didn't know the depth of it.

"I want to show you something that I think is going to mean something to you." He changed the shed all around and made it look like a little home. It was peaceful and nice, and I was amazed. I grieved that it was an exact opposite of what happened there. As a child, I desired an environment like this, but it never came. He said he knew that would make a difference to me. That's crazy that a kid I grew up with wanted me to see that things are changing for the good. He has three daughters and is dating someone who he is marrying. It is a whole different atmosphere of a dad and his kids than what I experienced. That was God answering my prayers that children would never get hurt and traumatized in that house and shed again.

I moved back there when I was older with my son who was a toddler and remodeled the whole inside of the house. After we moved in, I found a picture I had drawn as a kid on top of all their garbage. The people that lived there after us kept it. I was amazed.

When I went to the house and went through the rooms of where the trauma happened, I would speak to the rooms and rip out pages of the Bible and throw them in there. I yelled, "You can't have me! You can't have my brother! You can't have my sister!" The door slammed shut. I didn't know how to pray at that time, but just threw that stuff in there. My saying "it is done, it is finished" empowered me. Now the landlord's son is totally transforming the house placing bedrooms in different places and adding on rooms. It reminded me of how God was remodeling me.

I saw the landlord's son's mom. Every time she sees me, she cries for an hour and says, "If I would have known then what I know now, I would have helped you." She has a passionate heart. She didn't know the signs.

When I was being interviewed on a newscast, the interviewer wanted to go back to the old house where I lived. She asked, "What are the signs of abuse in which I should look?"

I told her and she started to cry saying, "I can't talk right now."

There were many times where God showed me love as a child. Mrs. Trowbridge lived across the street. She took us kids to Vacation Bible School one time. I learned Psalm 91 overnight. I quoted the whole thing when I went back the next day.

During this time is when I experienced God's grace in Jesus telling me that one day, He would come back for me, and that I would make the choice. I also thought about that when I was saved in 2001, when that woman who I had met at the gas station sang a song about an alabaster box and I went up front, I could feel that same love. I fell to my knees weeping and I heard His voice. I said, "You've come back for me." Jesus was the first man who kept His word to me.

I wish I could say that my trust in God was always solid, but it wasn't. It was a continual struggle. After my husband who was a Christian died in a car accident, I purposely gained weight; I was so scared that someone was going to traumatize me again, because I'm pretty. The thing

I feared most happened. I was raped a time after my car accident when I gained a lot of weight.

I believe God used that incident to show me I never deserved anything that anyone did to me. At the same time, I realized I didn't trust God for protection. I was honoring Him in every way except that, and like Job, the very thing you fear comes upon you. I made the decision that I wasn't going to be afraid anymore, but I still struggled with it. I didn't trust God with a lot of things. I realized it was not God's fault I didn't trust Him, it was my inability to believe in His promises.

When I started dating a good guy, I would find a reason not to be in the relationship, for I was unable to face the fear of being in one. I panicked and said I couldn't get married. I didn't see myself qualified to be in a relationship, nor could I see anyone truly loving me. Instead of being honest with myself about it, I spent a lot of time totally convincing myself and anyone around me that I planned to remain single, that I did not need a relationship. Truth be told once again, I didn't believe God's Word over my life. I ran from the truth.

I felt led by God to write letters to my future husband for the purpose of building my trust in God. In these letters, raw honest emotions of my heart to the man I had not yet known, but totally trusting in God to produce His promise. I would never do that if the man was already physically here. I know that one day when my husband reads these, it's going to be amazing. I didn't realize how much I needed a husband until that year. I thought that God had it covered and He would take care of me. I truly believed I didn't need a husband. He was saying that I am someone's rib and there is someone planned for me. I have to allow God to put that person in my life. It clearly is in God's Word that I am to be someone's wife. To rebel in words or actions to that is like telling God His Word is not true. So now I pray for my husband though it is not clear where he may be. I act in faith of seeking first the kingdom of God knowing all these things shall be added unto me. But it is clear I must put in action my faith and try, although trial and error are inevitable. The reality is I will never know unless I do. I am worthy to be someone's wife. I am perfect for him and that is what matters.

Dancing in Your Glory

By Malynda Osantowski-Hughes

Dancing in Your glory

Arrayed in Your unique design

Oh how I long for Your anointing oil

Pouring out of me from You,

Flowing out to whom You choose,

Oh the glory of You, my Lord

Your glory, Your embrace

Your presentation

Your invitation

Surrounded in Your glory

Surrounded in Your love

A walk, a run, a dance, my love

My first love, my very first love

My first love, my very first

Oh, I can still remember the recognition in me of Your first
kiss

The words You spoke were like a fresh raging river in me

The first time I realized You, You truly cared for me

A Father who cared for me,

No longer shall there be violence in your land, my kindness
shall never depart from thee. Your kindness overwhelmed

me, my Lord.

I can remember our first dance as if it were yesterday,

You took me into your inner courts

And showed me so many depths of You.

You taught me so much … that is the first day You taught me to walk with Thee,

At first it seemed I was so nervous and scared,

But so sure of the hand that held me near,

As I followed Your Holy Spirit's lead,

You would turn me to the left and then the right

Over and over

Around and around,

Closing my eyes surrendering to Your lead complete

Intimately growing in security in You,

Totally dependent upon you to lead me

Oh, the amazing embrace,

The morning kiss, the noon day love, the evening cascade,

the night engulfed in passion of Your agape love,

Awakening a new day

A new song

A reminder to me of Your unconditional love.

CHAPTER 10

My call to minister to others came from God. The words of the prophet Isaiah in chapter 61, verses 1 through 3, mirror what I feel my call is for Him.

The Spirit of the Sovereign Lord is on me,
because the Lord has anointed me to proclaim good news to the poor.
He has sent me to bind up the brokenhearted,
to proclaim freedom for the captives and release from darkness for the prisoners,
to proclaim the year of the Lord's favor and the day of vengeance of our God,
to comfort all who mourn,
And provide for those who grieve in Zion
to bestow on them a crown of beauty instead of ashes,

the oil of joy instead of mourning,

and a garment of praise instead of a spirit of
despair.
They will be called oaks of righteousness,

a planting of the Lord for the display of his
splendor.

This calling is not done in my own power. I could
never have been empowered with the teachings, healing,
and opportunities given to me to help others. It was all done
by God, but for a definite purpose. His plan is for me to
reach out to those who are in those dark places similar to
my experiences and to give them a hand out of the pit. God
has a plan for each person and He wants to shine light to
show them His great love. By exposing the darkness, the
shadows are weakened and the light of God takes over.

I am also called to equip others to help those who have
been trafficked or abused. The light shows them this is
happening; it is real. With that realization, they must then
know how to help victims. I am able to talk from the
viewpoint of a survivor, but I have been surrounded with
resources that are equipped to help victims regain the life
they were meant to experience.

God has placed the call right after my very own

biological son had suffered severe brain injury that wiped his memory of me and convinced him I was never in his life. One of the areas God laid on my heart is ministering to young men about my son's age. When God first began calling me to this, I was not willing to participate. This was a very hard command for me since I was missing my son so much.

God put one young man in my life who was like a puppy dog. He never went away and he would bring friends to me to visit. God used him to prick my heart. These were not young men out in the sex trafficking industry, but they were definitely heading to a serious at-risk in-road. The philosophy God gave me is if you can reach the life of one "dope boy," you can have a whole house of prostitution shut down! I knew I could not do this alone, but knew God could.

These young men had been abused or were struggling in another way. They began calling me Mama Bear. At first it was kind of annoying, so I joked with them if they called me "Momma Bear," I was going to call them Cubs. They just laughed, and it was their new nickname from me ... Cubs!

This ministry has grown so much. It started off with just a couple young boys hanging out with me in the summer of 2012. There's now 25 to 69 that gather together with me. They just keep coming back and hanging out. Individually, they would one-by-one share their life stories with me. That was neat, because they all had a lot of similarities in their lives, but none of them knew the struggles each of them were experiencing. Then when one would bring a new "cub," and they would say, "Momma Bear, you got to help this one." They found something in this group that they needed—love and acceptance. Somebody cared enough to listen. If people knew their stories and what they had endured throughout their childhood, then maybe they would understand the way they release the pain. Some of their stories are extremely horrific, and I will not put them in this book for others to read. Trust is important to victory in any of their lives. I have been entrusted with some of their stories and they are God's. It is only because they were never allowed the voice to speak.

There is a poem written by Antwuan Fishern that God used that to encourage me to answer the call he placed upon my life. It is called "Who will Cry for the Little Boy?" I highly recommend that you read it … it is powerful!

I would spend Saturday with the Cubs doing what they

wanted and listening to the music they chose, depending upon their music choice. It was my choice of opera or decent music on Sunday. Sunday would be my day and we would all go to church. We would then have a family meal together. As a group, they would just joke around.

I never shared my testimony about trafficking in this town where I live. This was my safe zone. I didn't talk about it. Then there was a news report of 105 kids rescued from trafficking. Fox 17 News wanted to interview me here. Julia Koch from the Hope Project arranged it. I wanted to drive there, but she said they wanted to come to where I live. I was swimming with my children and some of the Cubs from the group who were heathens and hoodlums back then, robbing stores, etc. just naughty kids. Fox 17 filmed me with all these kids.

I said, "They are all good kids."

One boy who heard that told me, "No one has ever called me a good kid."

Before I shared my testimony that day, the boys asked me why they wanted to interview me. I had to tell them the truth.

They said, "That's why you hang out with us, Mama Bear. You know what it's like. You've been there."

I said, "Yes, I also know what it's like to have nobody

there for you. I went my whole life never having anyone and said it is what it is. You guys are all family now."

Many of the boys are heavy into drugs to mask the pain in their lives, and I'm here if they need support to get off the drugs. One young man is very gifted in politics and I know God will use his voice. Another growing point for them is that the boys are starting to share their stories with each other.

Women at Risk International (WAR Int.) has helped multiply my efforts in helping others, along with The Hope Project. I have many opportunities to share my story. There are colleges that want to be a part of the answer in exposing the darkness. Every college to which I've spoken, I have kids coming up to me saying they have a friend going through the same type of experience. My heart is to get the information out and show them that there's safety, and people you can call that can deliver people out of these circumstances. Once people are aware, they are accountable.

I desire to bring awareness that organizations like The Hope Project are needed who are building safe houses for survivors of sex trafficking. The young women who are trafficked need to know that there's a safe place for them to go. So many are being rescued, but there's no place to bring them for treatment. They have so much going on inside that it is imperative to administer treatment as soon as possible.

While it is important to minister to the young women, the young men have just as many problems as I discussed earlier. Creating a safe house for young men to receive treatment is also very much needed. We don't normally think of the males being abused, but there are many.

My heart goes out to the other survivors who, like me, are older. They need to realize that they don't need to be ashamed. They can come out and boldly speak about it. The more we speak out, the more we move forward, standing up without fear against the man or woman who perpetrated us. Confidence is built as the truth is revealed. These young men and women who are survivors can take back control of their lives. It sends a clear message that the abusers can't hide it any more. I don't care if they are from family; they can't hide it anymore. Put the shame where it belongs.

As more victims come forward, the churches will need to be equipped for their treatment. Ministering to them is part of the healing process. Churches need to first accept that it is happening, more than likely in their community, and take steps to be equipped with what to do when they have a survivor in their midst. This is where information can be used in a powerful manner. Enlightening people about this subject, instead of keeping it in the dark, will empower them to be a part of the answer in ending this evil. Some of us may have to be vulnerable in sharing to give others strength to share.

The first time I shared my testimony was after my mother was in the hospital and I was at a yard sale for The Hope Project. I met Sue Martino, who is a leader there, and for some reason, I talked on and on about my experience to her because the clothes I was looking at for my kids were one dollar each and I was so excited about that. I had my kids with me and we were going out to eat. I remember I told her my testimony about my mom. I felt like thousands of pounds were lifted off of me. I didn't know what God was doing, but I never had that feeling before. For me, it felt like salvation and I wanted to keep telling people about it. She started smiling at me and had tears in her eyes.

She said, "Do you know what these clothes are for? We are selling them for the Hope Project."

"What's that?" I asked.

"It's a home we are trying to open for young women who are sex trafficked. Honey, you were sex trafficked."

"Really?" I didn't know what it was called.

"I would love for you to know more information and pray about it. Your testimony needs to be told."

It was amazing, because I watched the informational video when she came over with a man to talk with me about it. They said, "Show a testimony." This meant showing it through court and other official places. They also added, "You won't be able to talk about God."

I told her that I would pray about it, but I was pretty sure that God was the only person who helped me. I never had a counselor, I never had anyone else heal me, and God's supernatural way was what did it. I guarantee I'll tell somebody about it, and I wasn't going to do it their way. I prayed about it and God showed me Esther 2. She went in to the kingdom not really identifying herself with her people, the Jews, until the predestined time. So when I met with them again, I told them no. They came back a year later and said you can share your testimony any way you want. We want to do this.

I said, "Okay, I'm there."

When I first shared my testimony, it felt like I was talking in third person—I was talking about the other girl. It sounds crazy, but I had so much compassion for the other girl thinking, Wow, this is traumatic. Every time I shared my testimony, I got another dose of reality recognizing it was me and not some other girl. I remember the first time I shared at Michigan State University that it wasn't just about my childhood. I also talked about who I am today. Being the first time I shared this, it powerfully came through. There were 350 kids in the room and every one of them was crying and praying. They broke off into groups and started praying. I was amazed. In the midst of that, it registered that, "This is me, this is what happened, and this is what God has done." Look at how God brought me from the mass lies in which I lived.

Praise be His name!

Epilogue

I began working on this book a long time ago, and never did I imagine the ending of this book being what has become true in my life. I believe there is an importance of this final chapter. After all the traumatic history, what clearly is evident is the miracle working hand of God displayed in my healing, and strength through the struggles of where I showed endurance. The tenacity of gripping the hem and barely holding onto the garment of Christ. God was there when I at times had a hopeless outlook to my future, and being shown the harsh reality of being a soldier in God's army. There have been days on the battlefield I could barely stand in my armor, and days my armor fell to the ground and arrows hit me, serpents bit, and confusion hit me, but in the midst I was sustained only by God's amazing grace. My Rock, my all in all was all in all in me when I could be totally clueless to who I was, left me no choice but to hold onto the image of God. In Him was where I found me and discovered my life was not over … my life was not ended. In Him my life has for the first time just begun.

You will remember reading earlier in this book of a boy I had a crush on, but remained silent to him, because I thought so much of him that I never wanted him to know how horrific my life was then. The wounds I experienced kept me in a prison of shame. I couldn't speak out to him, even when he would walk up the driveway and flip his long blond hair with his hand. I would see him drive by in his white Monte Carlo. He was so amazing. He eventually got a girlfriend and I was sad.

The reason I write this, I was getting ready for my book to be published and I lost my step-sister to trafficking. I had to return back to the area I had been trafficked to prepare her funeral. I stayed with a cousin, and as I was leaving the driveway, I lost all use of my left side. I pulled into a church parking lot and immediately began praying. I called 911 and was taken to the hospital. There I discovered I had an aneurysm and was given a medication that the doctor made it clear to me I only had 10 minutes to take this medication or I could die, but also taking this medication could cause severe brain damage or paralysis. The nurse and I prayed and I chose to take the medication. I was then rushed to McClaren Macomb Hospital in Mount Clemens from Port Huron, Michigan, where I was in ICU for two days, then taken to a regular room. I was there two more days while the doctors continued tests on me. A 60 percent blockage went down to only 40 percent in two days. Hallelujah!

Although I survived, I was very discouraged. I couldn't drive for five days along with other restrictions and instructions given to me.

Feeling low, a little old lady came into my room and said the Holy Spirit instructed her to come in and say, "Honey, you know of Joyce Meyers?" She also listed other amazing women and then she said, "Honey, you are going to do greater things than they, and remember, God is going to bless you with an amazing breakthrough." She said the devil always tries to get in the way, and then she prayed with me and left.

I was still discouraged even hearing that word from God's messenger. I had been in prayer for one year as God directed me for a husband. The words she spoke seemed too far for me to reach … I felt hopeless. I was convinced I was put on earth to suffer and I will never live with a man who loves me as a husband and live happily ever after. I will never see my grandchildren and so on. I felt deflated.

As I thought about my children, I just wanted to get out of the hospital and take care of them, so I left. God made me go back and finish my stay.

When I was officially released, my son picked me up from the hospital and we went to my cousin's in Port Huron for the night to see how the funeral arrangements were going. I found out her body was being held for investigation. So I had my son take me home which was about four hours away.

About halfway there, the guy I had a crush on when I was young that I wrote about earlier, poked me on Facebook. Being "poked" on Facebook meant they just wanted you to know they were thinking about you without sending a message. This went on for a while and I sent him messages, but never received any response, only pokes. I became frustrated and after sending a friend request on Facebook, he responded to the message I sent about months prior. For some reason, he received that message from me that day.

I wasn't sure if I believed that, but then he asked me out on a date. I was shocked and his timing was bad since I was dying, hopeless and discouraged. We talked for hours.

He then showed up and instantly grabbed me and kissed me. That is where our relationship began.

We started dating and mind you the guy I once knew who was a hardcore, heavy metal, bar bouncing, bad boy, was now a man, though still walking strong in the same assurance of his own identity. He was determined and knew he was meant to be in my life. I am still thinking I am dying and now God sends me the love of my life? God, he's not even your son.

His name is Mark, and if you know Mark like I know Mark, I never pictured him a soldier of God. Then as I was sitting next to him on his bed, he was showing me his sleeves of tattoos. God gave me a vision of Ezekiel, prophesying to dead dry bones. He showed me the anointing upon Mark's life. We'll see what God does with this.

It amazes me that though my past surrounds me everywhere I go, and through all the trauma God has delivered me from, the familiar childhood places I see bring some happy moments to memory. Riding pigs or calves with my brother, going to church one time with a little old lady who lived across the street, and having an ice cream cone after a hard day's work with the landlords who lived nearby. I loved the smell of the fresh new house they had, and the amazing style of room they had for their daughter. I remember the joy of hearing the whooping sand crane that sat outside my window, the Weeping Willow tree that danced and bowed to her king all day and night. The adventures of digging to China. The smell of calf food and the kisses I received from the cows. The comfort of my pigs. The owl I nursed back to life. The times of running through the cornfields. The smell of fresh cut wood. The smell of a wood stove. The smell of fresh cut hay. I savor these good memories. Although these moments were small, they are significant to me because I can see them … I can embrace them.

It amazed me as a child to see things grow from a seed, and even occasionally I would see corn in the midst of the hayfield. Every seed provided exactly what it was made to do. Grass seed grew grass, and corn seed grew corn, and so on. It reminds me of God's Word. The seeds produced if planted, even near weeds, the hurtful things, and it helped me understand when God separated the wheat/truth from the tares/lies in me. It made me awake to see that in me were many seeds, but though many were bad, there was good seed and it produced a harvest in me.

As I write this, I sit not even a half mile from where my childhood trauma began. Ironically, my husband's friend is trading his trucks with us here.

I never would have dreamed of sitting so close and feeling so free, and reminiscing over some good memories.

But God knows how to turn ashes into beautiful things. Like receiving a message on Facebook to be friends with this girl whose name seemed familiar to me. I couldn't remember though since I lost a lot of memory in the car crash.

She sent me a message and said we were close friends in the sixth grade. She said we shared a locker, played on the playground, and rode the bus together every day.

I knew we had to be close because I normally didn't remember people that far back, but I remembered her name.

She asked me if she could ask a very personal question. I said yes, and so she asked me.

"Were you severally abused as a child? The reason I ask this was you would come to school in the summertime and you always wore long-sleeved shirts and pants when everyone else was wearing shorts. You cried all the time, but it was never when you got picked on. When that would happen, it was like it was normal to you. It was when people would be nice to you. You never ate lunch at school and you would hide in the bathroom. Well, I went in the bathroom one day and you were washing yourself off. I was bringing you my lunch and you freaked out. You kept screaming, "What do you want from me? What do you want?" I freaked out and cried with you. I did not know why you were so scared.

I went home that day and told my mom that we have to help you … we need have to go get you. But she said we couldn't.

Then the next day at school, a kid who was known as a trouble maker, put his hand on your shoulder and asked if you were okay. You screamed and cried and ran out of the room. It was then I went to the teacher because I saw your bruises and you smelled really bad. I knew you couldn't clean up the stains on your clothes. I had to tell the teacher, so I was the one who went to Mrs. Radwick and told her that the kid was being nice to you. I told her I really knew you were getting hurt at home, because you were really scared of people. I was afraid after that I would never see you again. I thought I got you in trouble and that you were dead somewhere. I was scared for years."

After reading her message to me, I wept for a long time. All this time, I never knew it was my friend, a school classmate who spoke up for me, and got the teacher to see something was wrong. It was not the only reason I was crying. It was recognizing someone had heard my cries and tried to answer them. I was so grateful and yet so sad to know all this time, she never knew what happened to me, and that she probably saved my life. Had the police never got involved, I may not be here today. I shared with her my gratefulness of what she did for me. I asked if I could share it in this book, to encourage other students that they could save a life someday, if they just watch and listen.

Only God could have made that connection and sent that angel to me in school to rescue me. Thank you, Jesus!

A LETTER FROM MALYNDA TO HER SIBLINGS

This is a letter to my dearest closest people to my heart, those who endured many waking moments of pain and even more than I ...

For years we were in seclusion from one another in control of the adults that surrounded us. We never communicated, unaware sometimes but yet aware, so deeply aware of one another's circumstances. In writing this book, I have done my best not to mention your pain, your hurt, and your feelings. Because even though our circumstances were the same, I know your story is yours to tell, and only you know how to define the way you felt. I would never assume knowing that.

As I write this letter to you, I want to share the Unspoken Bond we share stays with me. There is nothing I would not do to stop you from ever having to endure pain again. I can't stand to know you could be sad or hurting. I am and always will be there for you.

We have never shared with one another our true feelings of what has taken place in our lives. It's as if it was easier to keep the secret of the untold wounds that sunk deep in our souls, but yet managed to seep out creating havoc in our lives as we grew. Unable to fix it, it truly was easier to ignore. However, you never forget, you never forget the Unspoken Bond that is between us. I saw it when we got older and could help or do something about our circumstances. We were all willing to fight to protect the other from being injured. No more. If one was being hurt, we were willing to do whatever we could to help the other overcome.

When I began this journey with God, there was many times I was ready to quit. Life had so many hard circumstances let alone to keep letting Him tear open another would to remove the particles that hindered me from healing properly. If it wasn't for the speech our brother gave me in 2004 telling me that the horrific memories I was having were real, and sharing that my memories were nothing in comparison to all that actually happened, I might not be as far as I am in healing.

Brother, you remembered everything, every detail. You told me not to quit, to keep letting God do the work. You said you weren't ready yet, but you know how important it was for me to do the things for God. You reminded me that the truth of the matter was that it didn't make any difference how many good time parties I could go to here on earth, they could not compare to the party I will be going to in Heaven. You said that if I kept on, you would be there, too. From that day on, I chose to allow God to finish the work He had begun in me.

The next couple of years were major transitions in my life, and once again, life's circumstances hindered me from going forward. The love of my life was killed and my son critically injured. I did not know how to go on from there, and I was so angry at my loss.

You stood up for me and shouted, "If you quit now, what do I have?"

I was the only one you've seen walk the walk that I talked, and you believed in what God was doing in my life. You said, "If you quit, you would have nothing to believe in."

You spoke life to me in the midst of the storm. I bucked up and marched on. I am so grateful to you for never letting me quit. I love you and you are the most amazing person I know. Thank you for never quitting even when you could have with good reason. You kept going on and never looked back.

I am proud of the man you have become today. You are a husband, dad, and an awesome uncle. I will never cease praying for you. I know God has a plan for you and that your pain is real. I know your cries were true.

Thousands of children are going to be rescued from Child Exploitation, thousands are going to receive help to recover from the trauma that happened in their life. This is because you were God's voice to me when I needed it most. You encouraged me to share the truth of my life with others knowing that they may put two plus two together to discover who you may be, both you and my sister encouraged me.

The sounds of your silent screams echo in my soul and always will. I realize that your screams and mine are the real reason I am doing what I am today, for some other little boy or girl tormented the same way ... for all the children living life as we did. Their cries go unheard for years and no one knows what they are going through. I believe my truth this testimony will shed a light into the darkness and expose child sex exploitation and set the captives free. I want to thank you, my sister and brother, I realize that many of our views are broken and some damaged and buried deep, but all too evident are the words we hardly ever speak. The unbroken bond that say, I know where you've been, and there's no need to say, just know I am there for you and I will help you in anyway. We never had to say anything to one another, that unspoken bond spoke louder than words.

Thanks for encouraging me to stand up and share for children everywhere in the United States and all over the world. I am letting people know we have a voice and those silent cries are heard. Both of your voices matter to me. I

115

do not want other children enduring what we did and go without treatment and deal with the pain alone. Brother, your pain was never justified in the courts, and I so wish there was something I could do to give you that day, because you deserve to know your cries were heard.

You both endured so much; your pains were worse than mine and they were horrific. We have all overcome in our own way. You both are the strongest people I have ever known.

It was hard for me to ask you both about this book knowing the pain goes beyond words. I did not come forward to bring it up; I came forward so no other little child has to live their lives as we did. I am sorry for all that has happened to you both.

I was shocked when both of you supported me to keep going through healing, then to speak out, and then to write this book. If there is one thing that can propel a person is knowing that after all these years, the darkness, shame and pain of one's life can be transformed. It was your cries that hurt me so bad … I hated to hear your cries, to see how you both stand now and the odds you have overcome, that truly is the place I find strength and hope to do what I do.

I love you both, I really do and it's my honor to be your sister. It truly is for you both are survivors, fighters all the way. Come hell or high water nothing was stopping us from going forward. Thank you both for being there when I desired to quit.

Thank you, my sister, for being like a mom to me all those years. I pray that your life will be so blessed. I cannot wait to see it. You took a lot of the pain being older, and I don't know how you did what you did, because you did your best to try and stop what was going on. I remember just before I found out about knowing it was all wrong, you had punched one of the perpetrators right in the face. I will never forget that.

I am so grateful to both of you. Through the years, we have stood up for one another and whooping down anyone who even attempted to hurt one or the other. Then we grew up and now we don't fight physically to protect the other, but we pray and those prayers for each other have moved mountains. God is protecting each of us.

I love you both … you are the wind beneath my wings. I dedicate that song to you both. I love you. Jesus loves you for you both matter to Him.

Love your sister,

Malynda

PARTIAL LETTER TO MALYNDA'S PREDATORS

Dear Predator,

I was too small, too small to talk, too small to say no. I just barely walked and you tore my soul. You raped me and tormented me with torturous screams. I never knew any different then what you groomed me to be. You were my mommy and daddy, how could that have been? I found myself trying to be better at what you would request. The trauma was horrific even though it seemed I would escape deep within my mind, escaping pain, blocking the torment. I truly believed I was successful. I would await the hours that you or another would come into my room. I truly believed I must have passed the test and made my daddy proud. I even got so I wouldn't cry; I would just participate. I was never going to give you the satisfaction of seeing me cry. Sadly, I was just burying myself deeper and deeper inside. I no longer felt emotion. You did not like the fact I no longer would scream when you and your friends hurt me, but you knew how to make me wish I had, forcing me to be present when you would torture other little ones. You knew I hated the sounds of their screams more than my own. Oh, how I hated you for doing what you did. I could not even look at your other victim's without feeling ashamed. Wishing I was older and stronger, so I could make you leave them alone. All the days and nights, all the different men and the occasional women who would join in, it was torment that I thought would never end.

So many nights I laid there smelling the odor of your skins, the mixture of oil and bad body odors, a stench I will never forget. Forcing yourself upon me, making me swallow your excretions, and others. I never thought I would overcome or break free from what you had done.

Being set free in a field only to have to run like an animal as you and your friends would hunt me down like prey. I could never escape. I learned to hide my pain. I was strong and convinced myself that I would never let you know how much you hurt me and damaged my soul.

And mommy, deep inside I wondered, *Why did you hate me? Why did you call me a whore?* I did not understand and I could not see why for me to be good, I had to do things that inside I felt were so wrong. I never wanted to lay with those men, I never wanted to. You hated me and got mad and refused to hear my cries. I know you heard me, I know you heard the other children, but like a robot, I did what I was told. I remember when I refused, I was kicked in the head with a bottom of a shoe. You had no choice but to take me to the hospital and you said I had fallen. That's what you said, you lived the lies so much you forgot what was true. I could never understand, I hated the truth. When I was rescued from the horrific repetitive tormenting days from your man. You moved on to something new. I thought I was free, but it was not long till evil came over me again. All hope was gone, for years I thought you had won, damaged me for life. I went on to learn there are more men and women lived their lives like you. Selling an innocent child for something in return. I've seen murders, I've seen guns, I have seen what would happen if I did not want to perform sexual acts. It had become my identity. Who you created, who you wanted me to be ... your little whore. You stole my innocence, you tormented my soul. You know what you had done. For years, this went on until I was no longer yours to control. So sad because I knew I was damaged, I never ever dreamed of ever being whole, I never believed in love. I never believed in much of anything beyond this point until one day years later ....

I was hopeless and desperate; facing another failed marriage, my second child, and completely on the road to ruin. I began drinking all the time. I was trying so hard to numb the pain deep within my soul. I had grown weary of answers.

I was hanging out with a group of friends who did the same. It seemed as if we were all escaping from something. To open up to each other was something that happened only after we got too drunk to remember what it was that would spew from our mouths. It was going well until the day it seemed everything stopped. We all had just partied hard the night before and all of us got up and went to work as normal the next day. I was a construction worker at the time. Me and my brother were setting floor trusses in a motel building. We worked all day and went home to get cleaned up and pick my son up from his dad's home. I had a bad feeling inside about one of our friends we all hung out with. He was pretty upset the night before having confessed his love to a women he was in love with and she announced to him she was getting married. I had told a mutual friend of ours, but he felt I was just freaking for no reason. So I headed to go get my son. By the time I arrived at his home, I got a call on my cell phone. Seemed the friend I was concerned about had just committed suicide. He was one of the toughest guys I knew, fun, laughing all the time. He was friends with everyone, but like me, he was good at numbing and hiding the under current hidden pain and I guess he had enough and shot himself in the head.

I was so upset, I did not know God personally though I recognized He had to be somewhere. I just was not sure how to get to Him. I drove back that night just devastated. I was crying out to this God asking, "Why aren't you helping

120

us? Why did he have to die?"

The next day I spent just hanging with my son and daughter. When the weekend was over, I got up Monday morning to go to work, but I could not bring myself to do it. I got in my car and drove four hours away to a doctor's office that I knew would give me something to stop the hurt I was feeling inside. I was clearly aware that drinking was not going to remove this pain. I received the antidepressants and went to the store and bought some alcohol and began drinking while taking the medication. This was the only way I knew to numb the pain by self-medicating.

Then circumstances occurred that led me to Jesus Christ. The pastor that came to my friend's sawmill that day prayed the prayer of salvation with me and then baptized me in the creek. It was the best choice I have ever made.

Jesus has healed me from all the harm you have done to me. I am free now and living life to the fullest in the power of God. I am His daughter and He takes great care of me and loves me beyond understanding.

I have forgiven all of you for you will not own me in any way anymore. If I held on to bitterness, you would still own me. I refuse to let that happen.

In fact, I am praying that you can repent of your sins and accept Christ as your Savior. You no longer need to be a slave to your sin; you can be free like me, but it's your choice.

My life is now going to be wonderful thanks to God, who gets all the glory and praise for He is so worthy. He has given me purpose and I am living into it.

A daughter of the King,
Malynda

Malynda Osantowski-Hughes' theme of *Exposing the Darkness* is about helping people see the gripping reality of sex trafficking; it is no longer inescapable. Speaking out and giving a voice to those sex trafficked, Malynda shares her testimony of being trafficked in a small farming community through television, radio, training conferences, church workshops, and other organizations throughout the United States. Malynda works with organizations such as The Hope Project, W.A.R. International and the Michigan Human Trafficking Task Force. Her ministry, The CUBBS (Christ Uranium Blood Bought Soldiers) is for young men ages 16-24 who are at-risk.

Kathy Bruins is an author who has a passion for shining God's light of truth on the dark evil of human trafficking. She has other books out including *God's Daily Influence*, *The Book Proposal* with Kim de Blecourt, and *The Chronicles of Jake Tanner: Hell's Lane* with Neil Noriega. Kathy lives in southwest Michigan with her husband, John.

RESOURCE INFORMATION

Women at Risk, Inc. (WAR, Inc.), (616) 855-0796 or toll
free: (877) END-SLAVERY (363-7528)
www.warinternational.org,

The Hope Project: (231) 747-8555
http://www.hopeprojectusa.org/

Michigan Abolitionist Project (MAP):
http://www.michiganabolitionistproject.org/

Polaris Project: Tel: 202-745-1001
http://www.polarisproject.org/

TraffickFree: www.traffickfree.org

National Human Trafficking Resource Center Hotline

1 (888) 373-7888

Made in the USA
Middletown, DE
09 September 2015